The Lette

Trace and write the uppercase letter **A**.

Trace and write the lowercase letter **a**.

Circle each picture whose name begins with the short or long sound of a.

ant

zebra

apple

Adam

acorn

angel

The Letter Bb

Trace and write the uppercase letter **B**.

Trace and write the lowercase letter **b**.

Circle each picture whose name begins with b.

balloon

Bible

butterfly

squirrel

bus

banana

The Letter Cc

Trace and write the uppercase letter C.

C

Trace and write the lowercase letter c.

c

Circle each picture whose name begins with c.

hammer

cupcake

cow

camel

cat

jeep

The Letter Dd

Trace and write the uppercase letter **D**.

Trace and write the lowercase letter **d**.

Circle each picture whose name begins with d.

dog

donkey

David

donut

duck

pencil

The Letter Ee

Trace and write the uppercase letter **E**.

Trace and write the lowercase letter **e**.

Circle each picture whose name begins with the short or long sound of e.

turtle

egg

eagle

envelope

Eve

elephant

The Letter Ff

Trace and write the uppercase letter **F**.

Trace and write the lowercase letter **f**.

Circle each picture whose name begins with f.

fox

fan

bee

five

cake

fish

The Letter Gg

Trace and write the uppercase letter G.

Trace and write the lowercase letter g.

Circle each picture whose name begins with g.

gate

pig

Goliath

mouse

gorilla

guitar

The Letter Hh

Trace and write the uppercase letter **H**.

Trace and write the lowercase letter **h**.

Circle each picture whose name begins with h.

hippo

house

monkey

hammer

heart

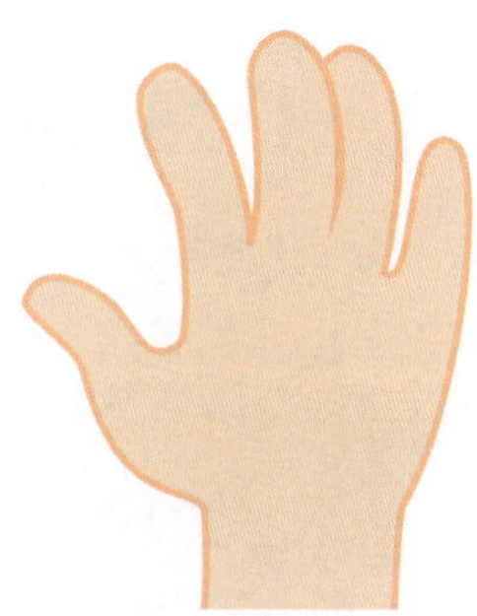

hand

The Letter Ii

Trace and write the uppercase letter I.

Trace and write the lowercase letter i.

Circle each picture whose name begins with the short or long sound of i.

mittens

igloo

iguana

island

ice cream

inch

The Letter Jj

Trace and write the uppercase letter J.

Trace and write the lowercase letter j.

Circle each picture whose name begins with j.

jar

snail

jet

Jesus

jeep

rainbow

The Letter Kk

Trace and write the uppercase letter **K**.

Trace and write the lowercase letter **k**.

Circle each picture whose name begins with k.

sun

wagon

king

kite

kangaroo

key

The Letter Ll

Trace and write the uppercase letter **L**.

Trace and write the lowercase letter **l**.

Circle each picture whose name begins with l.

leaf

octopus

light bulb

ladybug

lemon

lion

The Letter Mm

Trace and write the uppercase letter **M**.

Trace and write the lowercase letter **m**.

Circle each picture whose name begins with m.

mittens

mop

Moses

milk

monkey

bird

The Letter Nn

Trace and write the uppercase letter **N**.

Trace and write the lowercase letter **n**.

Circle each picture whose name begins with n.

net

nest

church

Noah

shoe

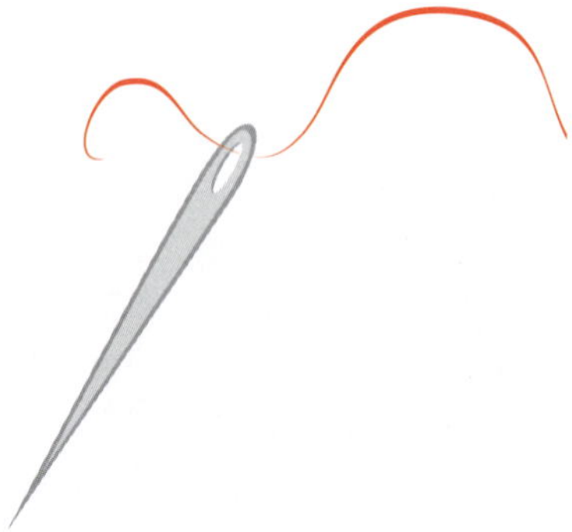

needle

The Letter Oo

Trace and write the uppercase letter **O**.

Trace and write the lowercase letter **o**.

Circle each picture whose name begins with the short or long sound of o.

owl

oval

overalls

cat

butterfly

octopus

The Letter Pp

Trace and write the uppercase letter **P**.

Trace and write the lowercase letter **p**.

Circle each picture whose name begins with p.

penguin

porcupine

pear

pumpkin

pig

ark

The Letter Qq

Trace and write the uppercase letter **Q**.

Trace and write the lowercase letter **q**.

Circle each picture whose name begins with q.

quarter

apple

quilt

queen

question mark

goose

The Letter Rr

Trace and write the uppercase letter **R**.

Trace and write the lowercase letter **r**.

Circle each picture whose name begins with r.

rose

scissors

ring

rainbow

kite

raccoon

The Letter Ss

Trace and write the uppercase letter **S**.

Trace and write the lowercase letter **s**.

Circle each picture whose name begins with s.

scissors

seven

sun

seal

sock

cross

The Letter Tt

Trace and write the uppercase letter **T**.

Trace and write the lowercase letter **t**.

Circle each picture whose name begins with t.

turtle

ten

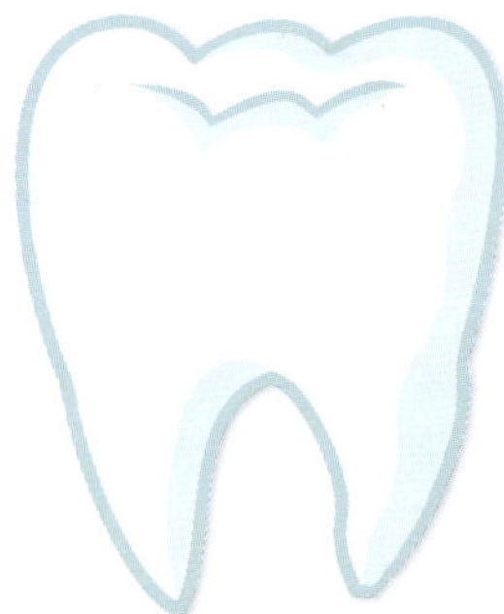

tooth

angel

teddy bear

lamb

The Letter Uu

Trace and write the uppercase letter U.

Trace and write the lowercase letter u.

Circle each picture whose name begins with the short or long sound of u.

umbrella

rose

crab

umpire

udder

unicycle

The Letter Vv

Trace and write the uppercase letter V.

Trace and write the lowercase letter v.

Circle each picture whose name begins with v.

vase

vine

owl

hippo

vacuum

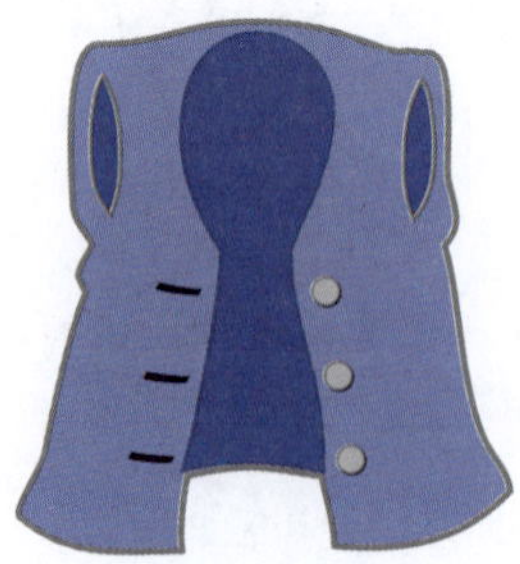

vest

The Letter Ww

Trace and write the uppercase letter W.

W

Trace and write the lowercase letter w.

w

Circle each picture whose name begins with w.

watermelon

window

wise men

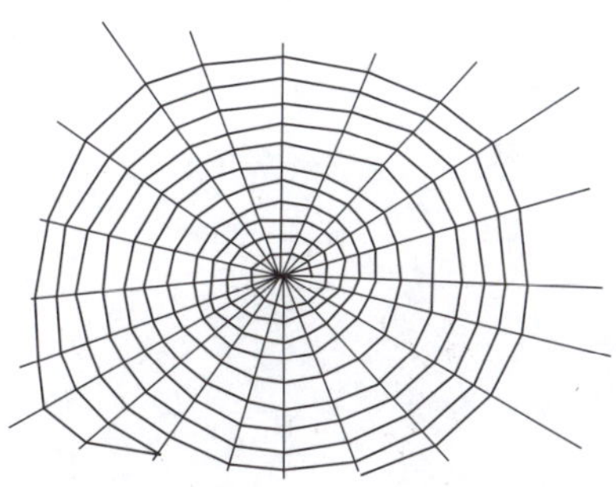

web

water

strawberry

The Letter Xx

Trace and write the uppercase letter **X**.

Trace and write the lowercase letter **x**.

Did you know that the letter **x** is usually heard at the end of a word? It makes the /**ks**/ sound like in **box** or **fox**. It can also make the /**z**/ sound like in **xylophone**.

Circle each picture whose name ends with the sound of x.

celery

six

wagon

raccoon

fox

box

The Letter Yy

Trace and write the uppercase letter **Y**.

Trace and write the lowercase letter **y**.

Circle each picture whose name begins with y.

yellow

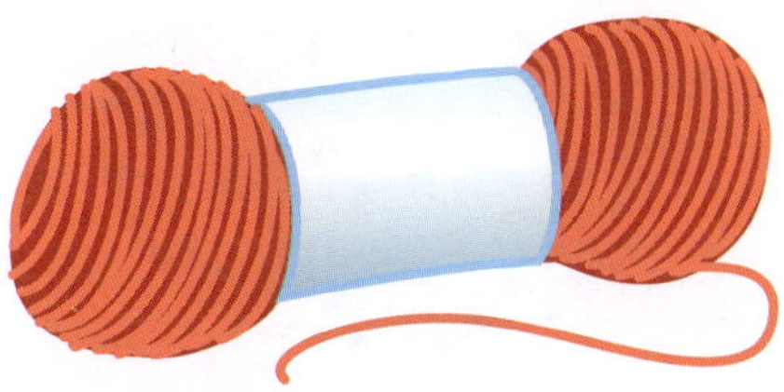

yarn

yolk

yo-yo

gift

yardstick

The Letter Zz

Trace and write the uppercase letter **Z**.

Trace and write the lowercase letter **z**.

Circle each picture whose name begins with z.

zero

whale

Zacchaeus

apple

zipper

zebra

Letter Partners

Draw a line to match each **uppercase** letter to its **lowercase** letter partner.

N	e
K	a
A	k
Y	q
E	n
B	y
Q	b

Letter Partners

Draw a line to match each **uppercase** letter to its **lowercase** letter partner.

H	h
M	y
J	p
G	j
P	q
Y	m
Q	g

Letter Partners

Write each **lowercase** letter next to its **uppercase** letter partner.

W		M	
P		A	
E		T	
B		R	

e t a b w p r m

Letter Partners

Write each **uppercase** letter next to its **lowercase** letter partner.

f		k	
x		q	
i		n	
g		d	

N I K X G Q D F

Letter Patterns

Circle the letter that comes next to continue the letter pattern.

e e F e e F	F e
g G g G g G	G g
A A a A A	a A
T Z Y T Z Y	Z T
B b b B b b	b B
h H h H h	H h

Letter Patterns

Write the letter that comes next to continue the letter pattern.

D d d D d d	
s S s S s S	
K L M K L M	
Q A Q A Q	
p C p C p C	
W m W m W	